THE ENTREPRENEURIAL GOD
A STUDY GUIDE

DONALD MCGILCHRIST

Global Commerce Network

2018

The Entrepreneurial God: A Study Guide
By Donald McGilchrist

Copyright © 2018 by Global Commerce Network

Global Commerce Network
P.O. Box 51455
Colorado Springs, Colorado 80949-1455
www.globalcommercenetwork.com

ISBN: 978-0-9970213-6-3
ISBN Ebook: 978-0-9970213-7-0

Cover Design: Rebecca Finkle
fpgd.wordpress.com

Editor: Glenn McMahan
endeavorliterary.com

Contents

INTRODUCTION

Most studies of the Scriptures start with a context. This helps us to stay focused even as we explore the grand themes of the Scriptures.

In these four studies, our context is enterprises. We choose this term to include commercial businesses, non-profit agencies, hospitals, consultancies, professional firms, and other forms of productive social organization.

Participating in the kingdom of God draws us to commit every aspect of our lives to the service of our king. Our enterprises, therefore, are more than "platforms" or "vehicles" for ministry; they should constitute ministry in themselves. They should not only be authentic and sustainable, but contribute to the *shalom,* or welfare, of their communities. Enterprises, especially commercial businesses, are highly relational in expanding the circle of stakeholders with whom we can enjoy fruitful and redemptive interaction. Enterprises should help people flourish and grow professionally.

These studies are designed to help entrepreneurs to anchor their work in the Scriptures and to strengthen their pursuit of their calling. Our model is God: creator, sustainer, redeemer, and king.

These four studies are focused on foundations rather than techniques. They are concerned with the significance, culture, and motivation of our enterprises more than the management of our enterprises. How do the Scriptures reveal and support the vital role that enterprises should play in helping workers flourish, and in improving the well-being of communities? Can our enterprises express of God's character and be part of his purposes?

A BEFORE-AND-AFTER EXERCISE

You will gain more from these studies if you first pause to think about your presuppositions. What is your understanding of the scriptural foundations of enterprises? Jot them down on this page.

As a concluding exercise, after you have worked through these studies, review what you wrote down here. How has the Spirit used the studies to influence your thinking? What has changed in your perspective? Do you have additional questions?

Gen 1:27-28
God created man in His own image

"Be fruitful, and multiple, and subdue the earth."
He invites us to be partners in His creation.

GOD'S ENTREPRENEURIAL VISION

The four studies in this book focus on what we can learn from God, the master entrepreneur. What did he intend? What is his strategy? How did he design us for this strategy? How did he handle opportunities and threats?

An entrepreneur is, literally, one who under-takes. He or she first has a vision. Then the entrepreneur launches the enterprise. It is sustained by the persevering commitment of the entrepreneur and the team. We are God's team.

Study 1 explores what God launched in his great undertaking. But what was his aim? What was he planning? As a visionary entrepreneur, what did he have in mind?

Before the beginning of time, our triune God—Father, Son, and Spirit—was functioning as what we may reverently call a planning group.

Just as the overture to an opera gives us hints of the drama that will unfold when the curtain rises, so there are several places in the Scriptures where we are given glimpses of God's vision and intent *before* creation.

EPHESIANS 1:3-6

Praise be to the God and Father of our Lord Jesus Christ, who has blessed us in the heavenly realms with every spiritual blessing in Christ. For he chose us in him before the creation of the world to be holy and blameless in his sight. In love he predestined us for adoption to sonship through Jesus Christ, in accordance with his pleasure and will—to the praise of his glorious grace, which he has freely given us in the One he loves.

2 Timothy 1:8-10

So do not be ashamed of the testimony about our Lord or of me his prisoner. Rather, join with me in suffering for the gospel, by the power of God. He has saved us and called us to a holy life—not because of anything we have done but because of his own purpose and grace. This grace was given us in Christ Jesus before the beginning of time, but it has now been revealed through the appearing of our Savior, Christ Jesus, who has destroyed death and has brought life and immortality to light through the gospel.

1 Peter 1:18-20

For you know that it was not with perishable things such as silver or gold that you were redeemed from the empty way of life handed down to you from your ancestors, but with the precious blood of Christ, a lamb without blemish or defect. He was chosen before the creation of the world, but was revealed in these last times for your sake.

Questions

What was the primary motivation that inspired God's entrepreneurial vision? How might his aim influence the way we think about our own entrepreneurial goals? *His overflowing love us, His desire for relationship with us.*

God's Overarching Plan

And what do we discover that God was planning? Our salvation, through Jesus Christ. The primeval chaos was not yet ordered, and human beings were not yet created. Sin had not yet entered the world, but God was already planning our salvation!

Hard though it is to comprehend, the Scriptures tell us that we were chosen, loved, graced, and redeemed before the world began. Why? There is an ultimate mystery surrounding God's purposes, but we know that he prepared for us the kingdom whose citizens would become followers of King Jesus.

We also know that his purpose was to reveal the riches of his grace, and to sum up everything in all creation in Jesus Christ. God desires us to flourish, to align ourselves with him, to relate intimately to him. God's innovation, the creation of the universe, was motivated by love.

Much more could be said—much is still hidden from us—but surely this at least is clear. The magnificent enterprise of God has always had, from eternity past, objectives that shape what follows in creation and redemption.

The overarching reality is that we were made to glorify God (Isaiah 43:7). We were chosen to be for the praise of God's glory (Ephesians 1:11-12). We are instructed to do everything for his glory (1 Corinthians 10:31). Here, then, is the focus and meaning of our entrepreneurial endeavors.

A Case Study
The Christian Worldview, Science, and Innovation

In his book *The Victory of Reason* (Random House, 2005), Rodney Stark documents how a Christian worldview was essential for science, universities, and entrepreneurship to develop and flourish during medieval times. Without a worldview that is based on the existence of a rational, personal God, there is no reason to believe that the universe itself is rational. If nature has no rational design or personal origin, then the systematic study of nature is undermined. Read the following excerpt from Stark's book (p. 14-16) and discuss the subsequent questions.

As Alfred North Whitehead put it during one of his Lowell Lectures at Harvard in 1925, science rose in Europe because of the widespread faith in the *possibility* of science . . . derivative from medieval theology. . . . He grasped that Christian theology was essential for the rise of science in the West. . . . [Whitehead said that this conviction] 'must come from the medieval insistence on the rationality of God.' To the extent that religion inspires efforts to comprehend God's handiwork, knowledge will be forthcoming, and because to comprehend something fully it is necessary to explain it, science arises as the 'handmaiden' of theology. And that's precisely how those who took part in the great achievements of the sixteenth and seventeenth centuries saw themselves: as pursuing the secrets of the creation. Newton, Kepler, and Galileo regarded the creation itself as a *book* that was to be read and comprehended.

For many renowned scientists in history, such as Newton and Galileo and Pascal, reasoned faith in a personal God compelled them to explore cosmology, astronomy, and physics. Many others, inspired by a Christian worldview, have improved the world through art, law, medicine, economics, and charity.

To what extent and in what ways has your view of God shaped and influenced your perspectives on work and entrepreneurship? How can you expand your understanding of God in a way that is integrated with your work, and what difference might this make in your business?

All God honoring, beautiful creation
Homes, jobs, etc is for God's glory.
If we pursue excellence with Him at the center
it is Missional Enterprise

THE ORIGINAL START-UP: LAUNCHING THE WORLD

Viewpoint of this Study:

God the Supreme Entrepreneur
Examining the Enterprise of God

God is good. He creates good things. He wants us to join him in creating good things. His son Jesus "went around doing good" and always did good things well. Acts 10:38 says, ". . . God anointed Jesus of Nazareth with the Holy Spirit and power, and . . . he went around doing good and healing all who were under the power of the devil, because God was with him."

In Mark 7:37 we read that, "People were overwhelmed with amazement. 'He has done everything well,' they said. He even makes the deaf hear and the mute speak.'"

In this study, we will reflect on God as the original entrepreneur, birthing new realities with the energy of his Spirit and the wisdom of his Son. Reading Genesis 1, what can we learn about launching an enterprise? For example: organizing, assigning functions, assessing quality. What more do you see?

GENESIS 1

In the beginning God created the heavens and the earth. Now the earth was formless and empty, darkness was over the surface of the deep, and the

Spirit of God was hovering over the waters.

And God said, "Let there be light," and there was light. God saw that the light was good, and he separated the light from the darkness. God called the light "day," and the darkness he called "night." And there was evening, and there was morning—the first day.

And God said, "Let there be a vault between the waters to separate water from water." So God made the vault and separated the water under the vault from the water above it. And it was so. God called the vault "sky." And there was evening, and there was morning—the second day.

And God said, "Let the water under the sky be gathered to one place, and let dry ground appear." And it was so. God called the dry ground "land," and the gathered waters he called "seas." And God saw that it was good.

Then God said, "Let the land produce vegetation: seed-bearing plants and trees on the land that bear fruit with seed in it, according to their various kinds." And it was so. The land produced vegetation: plants bearing seed according to their kinds and trees bearing fruit with seed in it according to their kinds. And God saw that it was good. And there was evening, and there was morning—the third day.

And God said, "Let there be lights in the vault of the sky to separate the day from the night, and let them serve as signs to mark sacred times, and days and years, and let them be lights in the vault of the sky to give light on the earth." And it was so. God made two great lights—the greater light to govern the day and the lesser light to govern the night. He also made the stars. God set them in the vault of the sky to give light on the earth, to govern the day and the night, and to separate light from darkness. And God saw that it was good. And there was evening, and there was morning—the fourth day.

And God said, "Let the water teem with living creatures, and let birds fly above the earth across the vault of the sky." So God created the great creatures of the sea and every living thing with which the water teems and that moves about in it, according to their kinds, and every winged bird according to its kind. And God saw that it was good. God blessed them and said, "Be fruitful and increase in number and fill the water in the seas, and let the birds increase on the earth." And there was evening, and there was morning—the fifth day.

And God said, "Let the land produce living creatures according to their kinds: the livestock, the creatures that move along the ground, and the wild animals, each according to its kind." And it was so. God made the wild animals according to their kinds, the livestock according to their kinds, and all the creatures that move along the ground according to their kinds. And God saw that it was good.

Then God said, "Let us make mankind in our image, in our likeness, so that they may rule over the fish in the sea and the birds in the sky, over the livestock and all the wild animals, and over all the creatures that move along the ground."

So God created mankind in his own image, in the image of God he created them; male and female he created them. God blessed them and said to them, "Be fruitful and increase in number; fill the earth and subdue it. Rule over the fish in the sea and the birds in the sky and over every living creature that moves on the ground."

Then God said, "I give you every seed-bearing plant on the face of the whole earth and every tree that has fruit with seed in it. They will be yours for food. And to all the beasts of the earth and all the birds in the sky and all the creatures that move along the ground—everything that has the breath of life in it—I give every green plant for food." And it was so.

God saw all that he had made, and it was very good. And there was evening, and there was morning—the sixth day.

Questions

1. The sequence and the actions God undertook in creating are instructive.
His enthusiasm for growth and diversity is contagious. He blesses
and takes pleasure in the richness of creation. This can inspire us to
exercise our creativity. How closely does your experience of launching an
enterprise align with what God did: his patterns, phases, and passions?

His rhythm and growth are calculated.
I can feel His joy in it

2. At the end of his creating, God "saw all that he had made, and it was
very good." What made his enterprise "good"? By extension, what makes
our enterprises "good"?

It is orderly.
It is beautiful.
It is beneficial to others.

BIBLICAL "JOB DESCRIPTION" FOR ENTREPRENEURS

Enterprises often fail because the original entrepreneur doesn't know
how to delegate and assign responsibilities to a team. However, God gave
us (his team) a clear job description. Seven verbs are used in Genesis 1:26-
28 and 2:15.

GENESIS 1:26-28

Then God said, "Let us make mankind in our image, in our likeness,
so that they may rule over the fish in the sea and the birds in the sky, over
the livestock and all the wild animals, and over all the creatures that move
along the ground."

So God created mankind in his own image, in the image of God he created them, male and female he created them. God blessed them and said to them, "Be fruitful and increase in number; fill the earth and subdue it. Rule over the fish in the sea and the birds in the sky and over every living creature that moves on the ground."

GENESIS 2:15

The Lord God took the man and put him in the Garden of Eden to work it and take care of it.

From these two scriptures, we find seven verbs that clarify our role as entrepreneurs. Take some time to thoughtfully address what each of these terms might mean in your context.

- Rule: What does this mean to you as a business leader?
- Increase: Why would God want us to increase?
- Subdue: In business, what does this mean?
- Be fruitful: What are some business terms for "fruit"?
- Fill: This implies there are empty spaces. Fill them with what?
- Work: How would you define work?
- Take care of: How are you caring for your environment even as you work to be fruitful?

Wayne Grudem adds: "Subdue (Hebrew: *kabash*) implies that Adam and Eve should make the resources of the earth useful for their own benefit, to develop the earth so that they could come to own agricultural products and animals, then housing and works of craftsmanship and beauty, and eventually buildings, means of transportation, cities, and inventions of all sorts."

It is not without significance that the Hebrew word for "work" in Genesis 2:15 (*abad*) is later used for worship. Work can be a form of worshiping God.

We are charged with extending God's great enterprise. As a good owner, he does not merely hand us the keys to the factory, but tells us explicitly what we are required to do. We are stewards.

Questions

1. Are these seven verbs apparent in your enterprise? What is lacking?

We are doing all. We could do all so much better.

2. Animals live off the generosity of God. Our task is to take nature (the capital base God provides) and to develop "culture." In Latin, this term helpfully links the spiritual (*cultus*) and the material (*cultivatus*). How are you working to enhance the culture of your enterprise?

Working to move my team to see that work both is worship.

3. Why did God assign to us these responsibilities? Does he need us?

He wants us to be in relationship with him as He creates.

No, He does not need us.

4. God created us in his own image and blessed us (Genesis 1:27-28). What does it mean to be God's image-bearers as entrepreneurs? For example, how should it impact the way we treat our colleagues?

As we work to be like Jesus we are to treat others as if they are Jesus.

5. What evidence in Genesis 1 and 2 supports the fact that we are made for relationship, partnership, community, and collaboration with our triune God and with one another?

The whole story is about our invitation to be His partner "image bearer" on earth as He completes His mission, His Kingdom.

A Case Study

The Loneliness Epidemic and Workplace Cultures

In the September 2017 issue of *Harvard Business Review,* an article by former US Surgeon General Vivek Murthy titled "Work and the Loneliness Epidemic" reports that over 40 percent of all Americans and over half of CEOs feel lonely. He adds that the high rates of loneliness in America are causing serious health problems.

"We live in the most technologically connected age in the history of civilization, yet rates of loneliness have doubled since the 1980s," Murthy writes. "People sit in an office full of coworkers, even in open-plan workspaces, but everyone is staring at a computer or attending task-oriented meetings where opportunities to connect on a human level are scarce."

Murthy argues that business leaders can and should play a vital role in changing workplace cultures as a means of combatting loneliness. This, he says, is because we spend most of our waking hours at work.

A second study reveals that 71 percent of American workers are so dissatisfied with their work that they are looking for new jobs. This survey of 17,000 people from nineteen industries, conducted by the nonprofit group Mental Health America and the Faas Foundation, found several factors that cause this problem. Chief among them was poor workplace relationships.

". . . 44 percent believe that they are 'always or often' overlooked. Sixty-four percent say their supervisors don't give them enough support and a majority of the participants are resentful of their co-workers. So much for teamwork," writes *Washington Post* journalist Gene Marks about the survey.

What ideas do you have for improving the relational aspects of your business culture? *Take time to listen. Ask questions.*

GOD'S ENTERPRISE REVEALS HIS CHARACTER

God didn't launch his great project, his "original start up," and retire. He actively supplies and sustains it. He is intensely invested in his creation. In so doing, his work reveals his character.

HEBREWS 1:3

The Son is the radiance of God's glory and the exact representation of his being, sustaining all things by his powerful word. . . .

PSALM 111:2-7

Great are the works of the Lord; they are pondered by all who delight in them. Glorious and majestic are his deeds, and his righteousness endures forever. He has caused his wonders to be remembered; the Lord is gracious and compassionate. He provides food for those who fear him; he remembers his covenant forever. He has shown his people the power of his works, giving them the lands of other nations. The works of his hands are faithful and just; all his precepts are trustworthy.

Questions

1. How does the way you lead your enterprise reveal your character, and how does your character influence your business? How can we grow in character, to better reveal God's nature in and through our businesses?

Spend more time in the word and prayer

COLLABORATION WITH GOD

God is continuing to work, and he tasked us to work with him. This collaboration can be seen in the next three scriptures.

PSALM 104:1-30

Praise the Lord, my soul. Lord my God, you are very great; you are clothed with splendor and majesty. The Lord wraps himself in light as with a garment; he stretches out the heavens like a tent and lays the beams of his upper chambers on their waters. He makes the clouds his chariot and rides on the wings of the wind. He makes winds his messengers, flames of fire his servants. He set the earth on its foundations; it can never be moved. You covered it with the watery depths as with a garment; the waters stood above the mountains. But at your rebuke the waters fled, at the sound of your thunder they took to flight; they flowed over the mountains, they went down into the valleys, to the place you assigned for them. You set a boundary they cannot cross; never again will they cover the earth. He makes springs pour water into the ravines; it flows between the mountains. They give water to all the beasts of the field; the wild donkeys quench their thirst. The birds of the sky nest by the waters; they sing among the branches. He waters the mountains from his upper chambers; the land is satisfied by the fruit of his work. He makes grass grow for the cattle, and plants for people to cultivate—bringing forth food from the earth: wine that gladdens human hearts, oil to make their faces shine, and bread that sustains their hearts. The trees of the Lord are well watered, the cedars of Lebanon that he planted. There the birds make their nests; the stork has its home in the junipers. The high mountains belong to the wild goats; the crags are a refuge for the hyrax. He made the moon to mark the seasons, and the sun knows when to go down. You bring darkness, it becomes night, and all the beasts of the forest prowl. The lions roar for their prey and seek their food from God. The sun rises, and they steal away; they return and lie down in their dens. Then people go out to their work, to their labor until evening.

How many are your works, Lord! In wisdom you made them all; the earth is full of your creatures. There is the sea, vast and spacious, teeming with creatures beyond number—living things both large and small. There the ships go to and fro, and Leviathan, which you formed to frolic there. All creatures look to you to give them their food at the proper time. When you give it to them, they gather it up; when you open your hand, they are satisfied with good things. When you hide your face, they are terrified; when you take away their breath, they die and return to the dust. When you send your Spirit, they are created, and you renew the face of the ground.

COLOSSIANS 1:17

He is before all things, and in him all things hold together.

1 CORINTHIANS 3:5-9

What, after all, is Apollos? And what is Paul? Only servants, through whom you came to believe—as the Lord has assigned to each his task. I planted the seed, Apollos watered it, but God has been making it grow. So neither the one who plants nor the one who waters is anything, but only God, who makes things grow. The one who plants and the one who waters have one purpose, and they will each be rewarded according to their own labor. For we are co-workers in God's service; you are God's field, God's building.

Questions

1. As you develop and operate your enterprise, how do you collaborate with God? In what ways has God participated with you in your enterprise?

God has brought us good people, great opportunities, Protection, customers. Everything at just the right time.

2. Entrepreneurship requires investment and risk. For example, many enterprises fail because they lack capital. How can we maximize the capital entrusted to us?

Have a well developed plan
Have a clear understanding of best cesead worst case scenarios.

Quotations

"Man is a maker, who makes things because he wants to, because he cannot fulfill his true nature if he is prevented from making things for the love of the job; he is made in the image of the Maker . . . and he must be himself or become something less than a man" (Dorothy Sayers, 1893-1957).

"The pursuit of commerce reconciles nations, calms wars, strengthens peace, and commutes the private good of individuals into the common benefit of all. . . . Commerce penetrates the secret places of the world, approaches shores unseen, explores fearful wildernesses . . . and with barbaric peoples carries on the trade of mankind" (Hugh of St. Victor, 1096-1141).

"The basis for determining the value of human work is not primarily the kind of work being done but the fact that the one who is doing it is a person . . . for when a man works, he not only alters things and society, he develops himself as well. He learns much, he cultivates his resources, he goes outside of himself and beyond himself. Rightly understood, this kind of growth is of greater value than any external riches which can be garnered. . . . Hence, the norm of human activity is this: that in accord with the divine plan and will, it should harmonize with the genuine good of the human race, and allow people as individuals and as members of society to pursue their total vocation and fulfill it" (Pope John Paul II, 1920-2005, *Encyclical on Human Work*).

"God himself loves the earth dearly and never takes his hands off it. And because he loves it and it is good, our care of it is also eternal work and a part of our eternal life" (Dallas Willard, 1925-2013).

"Work is not, primarily, a thing one does to live, but the thing one lives to do. It is, or it should be, the full expression of the worker's faculties, the thing in which he finds spiritual, mental, and bodily satisfaction, and the medium in which he offers himself to God" (Dorothy Sayers, 1893-1957).

"It is not only prayer that gives God glory, but work. Smiting on an anvil, sawing a beam, white-washing a wall, driving horses, sweeping, scouring—everything gives God some glory if, being in His grace, you do it as your duty. To go to communion worthily gives God great glory, but to make food in thankfulness and temperance gives Him glory, too. To lift up the hands in prayer gives God glory, but a man with a dung fork in his hand, a woman with a slop pail, give Him glory, too. God is so great that all things give him glory if you mean that they should" (Gerard Manley Hopkins, 1844-1889).

"Discerning the spirit or culture of a corporation is primarily a matter of testing its fruit. . . . Good cultures maximize the possibilities inherent in people and natural resources with regard to the widest ecological, societal, and temporal horizons. . . . Good cultures produce 'wealth' (a word linked to wellness or health) in the widest sense: they develop the potential of the natural world, they supply high quality goods at a reasonable price to those who need them, they embody an attitude of care to employees" (John Goldingay and Robert Innes, *God at Work*).

"Long before entrepreneurs see a return on their idea or investment, they must surrender their time and property to an unknown fate. They pay out wages even before they know whether their forecast has been accurate. They have no assurance of profit. . . . Entrepreneurs . . . serving the public and expanding the economic pie for everyone, can be counted among the greatest men and women of faith in the Church" (Robert Sirico, *The Entrepreneurial Vocation*).

"The specific work to be done—whether it is making ax handles or tacos, selling automobiles or teaching kindergarten, investment banking or political office, evangelizing or running a Christian education program, performing in the arts or teaching English as a second language—is of central interest to God. He wants it well done. It is work that should be done, and it should be done as Jesus Himself would do it. Nothing can substitute for that . . . as long as one is on the job, all peculiarly religious activities should take second place to doing 'the job' in sweat, intelligence, and the power of God" (Dallas Willard, The Divine Conspiracy).

"What God has given us is nature, whereas what we do with it is culture. We are not only to conserve the environment but also to develop its resources for the common good. . . . Our work is to be an expression of our worship since our care of the creation will reflect our love for the Creator" (John Stott, *The Radical Disciple*).

BUILDING ENTERPRISES IN A BROKEN WORLD

Viewpoint of this Study:

The Entrepreneurial God Encounters Turbulence
Working with a Dysfunctional Team

The darkest day for God's team came quickly. Adam and Eve chose to disobey God:

- by forgetting their origins . . . how they were created
- by disgracing his image . . . how they were designed
- by ignoring his requirements . . . how they were tasked
- by rejecting his provision . . . how they were sustained
- by spurning his favor . . . how they were blessed

We all share in the primal sin described in the garden. Our prideful turn away from God naturally separated us from him, from one another, and from all that God had made. All of our relationships were damaged. We lost innocence, intimacy, and initiative. We acquired division, drudgery, and death. Our connectedness to God turned into painful isolation. Our identity was compromised. The consequences of pride spread everywhere. Indeed, the universe became abnormal. The world no longer functions according to specification.

The pattern of human disobedience proved unshakable without Christ. We are still in rebellion. We are damaged. We cannot fix ourselves. In your opinion, what was broken? How has this infected your enterprise?

Instead of trusting God to be our partner we tried to seize control.

THE DESCENT OF HUMANKIND

Sin is idolatry. It replaces the reign of God in our hearts with destructive attractions and futile desires. Analyze the descent of humankind as described in the scriptures below.

GENESIS 3:17-19

Cursed is the ground because of you; through painful toil you will eat food from it all the days of your life. It will produce thorns and thistles for you, and you will eat the plants of the field. By the sweat of your brow you will eat your food until you return to the ground, since from it you were taken; for dust you are and to dust you will return.

ROMANS 1:20-25

For since the creation of the world God's invisible qualities—his eternal power and divine nature—have been clearly seen, being understood from what has been made, so that people are without excuse. For although they knew God, they neither glorified him as God nor gave thanks to him, but their thinking became futile and their foolish hearts were darkened. Although they claimed to be wise, they became fools and exchanged the glory of the immortal God for images made to look like a mortal human being and birds and animals and reptiles. Therefore God gave them over in the sinful desires of their hearts to sexual impurity for the degrading of their bodies with one another. They exchanged the truth about God for a lie, and worshiped and served created things rather than the Creator—who is forever praised. Amen.

Questions

1. What are some temptations to which we as leaders of enterprises are especially prone? In what ways do our struggles with sin create problems in our businesses? *Pride*

GOD'S PERSISTENCE

Given the cancerous spread of sin, how did God first respond? In Genesis 6, we see God's anguish over the failure of his team, the disruption of his project. However, in his mercy, God decided instead to work with a new team and to draw up for them a revised contract or covenant (Genesis 9:8-17). What other observations do you have about God's revised strategy?

GENESIS 6:5-7

The Lord saw how great the wickedness of the human race had become on the earth, and that every inclination of the thoughts of the human heart was only evil all the time. The Lord regretted that he had made human beings on the earth, and his heart was deeply troubled. So the Lord said, "I will wipe from the face of the earth the human race I have created—and with them the animals, the birds and the creatures that move along the ground—for I regret that I have made them."

GENESIS 9:8-17

Then God said to Noah and to his sons with him: "I now establish my covenant with you and with your descendants after you and with every living creature that was with you—the birds, the livestock and all the wild animals, all those that came out of the ark with you—every living creature on earth. I establish my covenant with you: Never again will all life be destroyed by the waters of a flood; never again will there be a flood to destroy the earth."

And God said, "This is the sign of the covenant I am making between me and you and every living creature with you, a covenant for all generations to come: I have set my rainbow in the clouds, and it will be the sign of the covenant between me and the earth. Whenever I bring clouds over the earth and the rainbow appears in the clouds, I will remember my covenant between me and you and all living creatures of every kind. Never again will the waters become a flood to destroy all life. Whenever the rainbow appears in the clouds, I will see it and remember the everlasting covenant between God and all living creatures of every kind on the earth."

So God said to Noah, "This is the sign of the covenant I have established between me and all life on the earth."

Questions

1. In light of God's astonishing persistence, what "takeaways" from these scriptures will help you lead your enterprise?

God will be faithful and persistent in working through our business to reach people. It would be wise to partner with him on that journey.

2. In the scriptures above, God clearly takes a stand against evil and its destructiveness. What does this imply for A) your own role as a leader and B) the way you deal with your co-workers and employees?

I must take a stand for light and creativity.

DANGEROUS PITFALLS

As entrepreneurs, we make plans, we face intense competition, and we employ workers. Sometimes, the "system" in which we work is rife with corruption. These conditions expose us to danger and traps.

JAMES 4:1-5:9

What causes fights and quarrels among you? Don't they come from your desires that battle within you? You desire but do not have, so you kill. You covet but you cannot get what you want, so you quarrel and fight. You do not have because you do not ask God. When you ask, you do not receive, because you ask with wrong motives, that you may spend what you get on your pleasures.

You adulterous people, don't you know that friendship with the world means enmity against God? Therefore, anyone who chooses to be a friend of the world becomes an enemy of God. Or do you think Scripture says without reason that he jealously longs for the spirit he has caused to dwell in us? But he gives us more grace. That is why Scripture says:

"God opposes the proud but shows favor to the humble." Submit yourselves, then, to God. Resist the devil, and he will flee from you. Come near to God and he will come near to you. Wash your hands, you sinners, and purify your hearts, you double-minded. Grieve, mourn and wail. Change your laughter to mourning and your joy to gloom. Humble yourselves before the Lord, and he will lift you up.

Brothers and sisters, do not slander one another. Anyone who speaks against a brother or sister or judges them speaks against the law and judges it. When you judge the law, you are not keeping it, but sitting in judgment on it. There is only one Lawgiver and Judge, the one who is able to save and destroy. But you—who are you to judge your neighbor?

Now listen, you who say, "Today or tomorrow we will go to this or that city, spend a year there, carry on business and make money." Why, you do not even know what will happen tomorrow. What is your life? You are a mist that appears for a little while and then vanishes. Instead, you ought to say, "If it is the Lord's will, we will live and do this or that." As it is, you boast in your arrogant schemes. All such boasting is evil. If anyone, then, knows the good they ought to do and doesn't do it, it is sin for them.

Now listen, you rich people, weep and wail because of the misery that is coming on you. Your wealth has rotted, and moths have eaten your clothes. Your gold and silver are corroded. Their corrosion will testify against you and eat your flesh like fire. You have hoarded wealth in the last days. Look! The wages you failed to pay the workers who mowed your fields are crying out against you. The cries of the harvesters have reached the ears of the Lord Almighty. You have lived on earth in luxury and self-indulgence. You have fattened yourselves in the day of slaughter. You have condemned and murdered the innocent one, who was not opposing you.

Be patient, then, brothers and sisters, until the Lord's coming. See how the farmer waits for the land to yield its valuable crop, patiently waiting for the autumn and spring rains. You too, be patient and stand firm, because the Lord's coming is near. Don't grumble against one another, brothers and sisters, or you will be judged. The Judge is standing at the door!

Questions

1. List several of the negative behaviors James mentions that can easily gain a foothold in your enterprise. How might his exhortations help you?

Desires, Quarrels, Pride, friendship with the World Hoarding wealth. Not treating others fairly.

Pursue God first. Be patient. Trust Him.

2. James warns us against boasting and the delusions that accompany commercial success. This is not a new problem. What remedies do you propose for our pride?

Practice giving compliments to others.
Practice generosity.
Read the Word / Listen to others.

THE CORE PROBLEM: PRIDE

Let's also look at the impact of our pride in commerce. Consider the first great urban construction project, Babel (Genesis 11:1-9), and the testimony of Solomon, one of the greatest entrepreneurs and builders (Ecclesiastes 2:4-11).

GENESIS 11:1-9

Now the whole world had one language and a common speech. As people moved eastward, they found a plain in Shinar and settled there.

They said to each other, "Come, let's make bricks and bake them thoroughly." They used brick instead of stone, and tar for mortar. Then they said, "Come, let us build ourselves a city, with a tower that reaches to the heavens, so that we may make a name for ourselves; otherwise we will be scattered over the face of the whole earth."

But the Lord came down to see the city and the tower the people were building. The Lord said, "If as one people speaking the same language they have begun to do this, then nothing they plan to do will be impossible for them. Come, let us go down and confuse their language so they will not understand each other."

So the Lord scattered them from there over all the earth, and they stopped building the city. That is why it was called Babel—because there the Lord confused the language of the whole world. From there the Lord scattered them over the face of the whole earth.

ECCLESIASTES 2:4-11

I undertook great projects: I built houses for myself and planted vineyards. I made gardens and parks and planted all kinds of fruit trees in them. I made reservoirs to water groves of flourishing trees. I bought male and female slaves and had other slaves who were born in my house. I also owned more herds and flocks than anyone in Jerusalem before me. I amassed silver and gold for myself, and the treasure of kings and provinces. I acquired male and female singers, and a harem as well—the delights of a man's heart. I became greater by far than anyone in Jerusalem before me. In all this my wisdom stayed with me.

I denied myself nothing my eyes desired; I refused my heart no pleasure. My heart took delight in all my labor, and this was the reward for all my toil. Yet when I surveyed all that my hands had done and what I had toiled to achieve, everything was meaningless, a chasing after the wind; nothing was gained under the sun.

Questions

1. What was at fault in these projects? What can we learn from Solomon's assessment of his self-oriented "toil"?

God was not at center.
Pursuing God first is the only answer.

A Case Study
Tyre and Babylon

As entrepreneurs, we lead our businesses in a cultural and political context. Tyre was the most entrepreneurial and commercial city described in the Old Testament. She was "the marketplace of the nations" (Isaiah 23:3). She was a cultural and cosmopolitan megacity. When we map the trade routes that she used and the sources from which she assembled her magnificent ships, we discover that her traders were active in what was then the known world.

God welcomed the initiative of her citizens as they pursued the seven verbs of Genesis 1 and 2. "When your merchandise went out on the seas, you satisfied many nations; with your great wealth and your wares, you enriched the kings of the earth" (Ezekiel 27:33). Indeed, Tyre's energies are described in terms that are similar to the vibrant commercial activity that will characterize the last days.

Yet, Tyre's citizens eventually succumbed to the same sins that can easily undermine our enterprises today. Study their story in Isaiah 23 and Ezekiel 27 and 28.

Babylon was another trading megacity. Exorbitant prosperity was built on abusive slavery. Her commercial success was driven by oppression. Revelation 18:11-13 describes Babylon this way:

> The merchants of the earth will weep and mourn over her because no one buys their cargoes anymore—cargoes of gold, silver, precious stones and pearls; fine linen, purple, silk and scarlet cloth; every sort of citron wood, and articles of every kind made of ivory, costly wood, bronze, iron and marble; cargoes of cinnamon and spice, of incense, myrrh and frankincense, of wine and olive oil, of fine flour and wheat; cattle and sheep; horses and carriages; and human beings sold as slaves.

How does today's global commerce compare to Babylon and Tyre?

Greed, pride, and taking advantage of others.

A Case Study
The Brazilian Janitor

Many entrepreneurs must attempt to start and sustain businesses in corrupt economic systems. Bribery, money laundering, and even violence make it difficult for honest entrepreneurs to keep companies afloat.

According to Transparency International, "The effect of corruption on the social fabric of society is the most damaging of all. It undermines people's trust in the political system, in its institutions and its leadership. Frustration and general apathy among a disillusioned public result in a weak civil society."

A story from Brazil reminds us of the importance of integrity, even when it is difficult. A multi-billion dollar corruption scandal involving high-level politicians and multinational corporations was wreaking economic havoc. As Brazilian media unveiled this ruinous corruption, a major newspaper published a story about an honest airport janitor. The story went viral.

While Francisco Cavalcante cleaned a bathroom at the Brasilia airport, something he'd done every day for twenty-six years, he found a bag with $10,000 inside. This was a lot of money for anyone, but especially for Cavalcante, who earned only $120 a month at the time. That $10,000 was equal to seven years of the janitor's wages!

The bag also contained a passport belonging to a Swiss tourist. So now Cavalcante had a private decision to make: keep the money or try to return it to the owner. He chose to turn the money over to the authorities who, thankfully, returned the money to its rightful owner.

Cavalcante's decision inspired the entire country during a time when Brazilians had lost hope. He became, at least for a while, a national hero.

"What I did was what everyone should do," said Cavalcante when interviewed by a journalist. "If everyone did this, Brazil would be a better place. And there's nothing better in life than to come home and sleep with a clear conscience. . . . This is all I want for my family and me."

As you consider Cavalcante's values and choices, what do you see that corresponds with what we have read in the Scriptures about building enterprises in a broken world? In the context of a competitive, hardball business climate, can honest and mild-mannered business leaders survive?

Well, yes and no. An honest business can have impact and legacy — even if it may be unable to survive economic conditions.

CHARACTER AND ENTERPRISES

Entrepreneurship is fundamentally relational. Enterprises bring people together. They require teamwork to survive. In this relational context, there is a tension. Because people are sinful, we are inclined to selfishness and arrogance. Because we are created in the image of God, we are capable of goodness and love.

Thus, our work can be pleasing to God. As we see in the life of Nehemiah, our concern for the needs of people can compel us to serve others through our work. Notice the compassionate heart of Nehemiah, a prominent leader during Israel's years in exile.

"They said to me [Nehemiah], 'Those who survived the exile and are back in the province are in great trouble and disgrace. The wall of Jerusalem is broken down, and its gates have been burned with fire.' When I heard these things, I sat down and wept. For some days I mourned and fasted and prayed before the God of heaven" (Nehemiah 1:3-4).

Nehemiah's compassion for people (he mourned for days) led him to act. You can read more about Nehemiah's courageous work in chapters 2:4 to 7:3) as he rebuilds the walls of Jerusalem. The project was a classic entrepreneurial challenge.

Another example of our capacity for goodness can be found in the portrait of the virtuous woman, in Proverbs 31. This is a paean of praise for a person of energy and initiative. Read this chapter and describe what you see in her that you would like to emulate.

GROWING IN CHARACTER

Although we are deeply flawed, God calls us to become more and more like him in our character. We do this with *his* help, not according to *self*-help. In his grace, and as we respond in humility to his guidance, he gives us the ability to grow.

As entrepreneurs on God's team, we can study the lives and virtues of godly leaders. For example, we can learn much from the perseverance of Job, the trustworthiness of Joseph, and the courage of David. The apostle Paul refers to soldiers, athletes, and farmers as examples of endurance and commitment. These people demonstrate some of the qualities that distinguish successful entrepreneurs.

2 TIMOTHY 2:4-6

No one serving as a soldier gets entangled in civilian affairs, but rather tries to please his commanding officer. Similarly, anyone who competes as an athlete does not receive the victor's crown except by competing according to the rules. The hardworking farmer should be the first to receive a share of the crops.

1 CORINTHIANS 9:24-26

Do you not know that in a race all the runners run, but only one gets the prize? Run in such a way as to get the prize. Everyone who competes in the games goes into strict training. They do it to get a crown that will not last, but we do it to get a crown that will last forever. Therefore I do not run like someone running aimlessly; I do not fight like a boxer beating the air.

PHILIPPIANS 2:3-4, 14-15

Do nothing out of selfish ambition or vain conceit. Rather, in humility value others above yourselves, not looking to your own interests but each of you to the interests of the others. . . . Do everything without grumbling or arguing, so that you may become blameless and pure, "children of God without fault in a warped and crooked generation." Then you will shine among them like stars in the sky . . .

2 PETER 1:3-8

His divine power has given us everything we need for a godly life

through our knowledge of him who called us by his own glory and goodness. Through these he has given us his very great and precious promises,
so that through them you may participate in the divine nature, having es-
caped the corruption in the world caused by evil desires. . . . Make every
effort to add to your faith goodness; and to goodness, knowledge; and to
knowledge, self-control; and to self-control, perseverance; and to perseverance, godliness; and to godliness, mutual affection; and to mutual affection, love. For if you possess these qualities in increasing measure, they
will keep you from being ineffective and unproductive in your knowledge
of our Lord Jesus Christ.

Questions

1. What is required to grow in these vital character traits? In addition to
what's described in the scriptures above, what qualities do you think are
essential for entrepreneurs?

Walking with and looking to Jesus.

Patience + Trust

2. What relationship do you see between these qualities and a successful
enterprise? Do they provide a guarantee of success?

⟿ a great deal   *⟿ No - circumstances*
                          outside of our control

GOD'S INVESTMENT IN US

God gives us the ability to excel. He not only helps us grow in virtue
and character, he provides the resources we need. He favors us with his
generosity. "Unless the Lord builds the house, its builders labor in vain"

(Psalm 127:1).

God is not an absentee owner. In fact, he stays invested in every detail of our work. Consider the agricultural techniques described in Isaiah 28:23-29, shown below. Notice God's attention to detail in partnership with us.

Another example is found in Exodus 31:1-11, which highlights the first person in the Scriptures who is described as filled with the Spirit of God. Bezalel was a craftsman, not a prophet or priest or king. Again, we recognize God's concern for beauty as well as functionality.

We need the support, ability, gifting, restoration, and redemption that only Christ can provide. "May the favor of the Lord our God rest upon us; establish the work of our hands for us—yes, establish the work of our hands" (Psalm 90:17).

Isaiah 28:23-29

Listen and hear my voice; pay attention and hear what I say. When a farmer plows for planting, does he plow continually? Does he keep on breaking up and working the soil? When he has leveled the surface, does he not sow caraway and scatter cumin? Does he not plant wheat in its place, barley in its plot, and spelt in its field? His God instructs him and teaches him the right way. Caraway is not threshed with a sledge, nor is the wheel of a cart rolled over cumin; caraway is beaten out with a rod, and cumin with a stick. Grain must be ground to make bread; so one does not go on threshing it forever. The wheels of a threshing cart may be rolled over it, but one does not use horses to grind grain. All this also comes from the Lord Almighty, whose plan is wonderful, whose wisdom is magnificent.

Exodus 31:1-11

Then the Lord said to Moses, "See, I have chosen Bezalel son of Uri, the son of Hur, of the tribe of Judah, and I have filled him with the Spirit of God, with wisdom, with understanding, with knowledge and with all kinds of skills—to make artistic designs for work in gold, silver and bronze, to cut and set stones, to work in wood, and to engage in all kinds of crafts. More-over, I have appointed Oholiab son of Ahisamak, of the tribe of Dan, to help him. Also I have given ability to all the skilled workers to make everything I have commanded you: the tent of meeting, the ark of the covenant law with the atonement cover on it, and all the other furnishings of the tent—the ta-ble and its articles, the pure gold lampstand and all its accessories, the altar of incense, the altar of burnt offering and all its utensils, the basin with its stand—and also the woven garments, both the sacred garments for Aaron the priest and the garments for his sons when they serve as priests, and the anointing oil and fragrant incense for the Holy Place. They are to make them just as I commanded you."

Questions

1. Isaiah 28 refers to the wisdom and knowledge needed to run an enterprise. Exodus 31 emphasizes the need for skill, talent, and gifting. What happens if only one or the other is present in a leader? In today's dynamic economy, which is most valued in workers?

Skill & talent seemed to be most valued in our secular economy. Short-sighted

Quotations

"The life of the godly is justly compared to trading, for they ought nat-urally to exchange and barter with one another in order to maintain inter-course" (John Calvin, 1509-1564).

"Micah's . . . three statements of responsibility—do justice, love mercy, walk humbly with your God—are demands that working Christian manag-ers should be using to measure each business decision they make, especially in the context of its impact on their employees. . . . Christian managers owe our allegiance to the God who sacrificed his Son for their eternal security, and for their present comfort. And what does God require of us . . . that the very acts we engage in, the very principles we rely on, the very decisions we make, not be in service to ourselves, but in service to those around us, doing justice, loving mercy and demonstrating clearly to them just how glad we are to be walking where God walks. It's time for the corner office to serve the cubicles again" (Randy Kilgore, Marketplace Network on Micah 6:6-8).

"Kingdom business professionals . . . seek to influence employees, partners, suppliers, customers, and the local community for Christ. They use business itself to demonstrate biblical business principles and set values. They serve others through quality products and helpful services. They seek to provide a venue for people to use their gifts and earn a living. They desire to create a culture of light in and around the businesses that they develop through good, biblically based business principles and the love of Jesus Christ" (Ken Eldred, *God is at Work*).

". . . God calls us to himself so decisively that everything we are, everything we do, and everything we have is invested with a special devotion and dynamism lived out as a response to his summons and service" (Os Guinness, *The Call*).

". . . the church has historically treated business with some distaste, failing to recognize that the poor need jobs, not just aid, and that there is no poverty alleviation without wealth generation. As one businessman put it: 'The church appreciates my tithe but not the enterprise that gives rise to it.' The abundant life in Jesus involves living as material human beings. We're called to work with God to make the world a better place, to produce goods and services that benefit people to the glory of God, to alleviate poverty by creating jobs as well as offering aid, to work to release potential through endeavor—sand into silicon chips, children into confident adults, disparate individuals into productive teams" (Mark Greene, *The Great Divide*).

"Any enterprise built by wise planning becomes strong through common sense, and profits wonderfully by keeping abreast of the facts" (Proverbs 24:3-4, TLB).

"In nothing has the Church so lost her hold on reality as in her failure to understand and respect the secular callings. She has allowed work and religion to become separate departments, and is astonished to find that, as a result, the secular work of the world has turned to selfish and destructive ends, and that the greater part of the world's intelligent workers have become irreligious, or at least, uninterested in religion" (Dorothy Sayers, 1893-1957).

"Our people must learn to devote themselves to doing what is good, in order to provide for urgent needs and not live unproductive lives" (Titus 3:14).

"All these rely on their hands, and each is skillful at his own craft. Without them a city would have no inhabitants; no settlers or travelers would come to it. Yet they are not in demand at public discussions or prominent in the assembly. They do not sit on the judge's bench or understand the decisions of the courts. They cannot expound moral or legal principles and are not ready with maxims. But they maintain the fabric of this world, and their daily work is their prayer" (Ben Sira, in Ecclesiasticus 38:31-34, a book much used in the early Christian Church but excluded as Apocrypha by the Protestant Reformers).

"The very good thing that is a market economy becomes the very bad thing that is a market society when culture is taken captive to whatever can attract a paying crowd" (Richard John Neuhaus, 1936-2009).

ENTERPRISES AND THE GOSPEL

Viewpoint of this Study

God, the Committed Entrepreneur
Modeling – Training – Resourcing – Sacrificing

As we have seen, despite our prideful pursuit of autonomy, God works to recover our allegiance. His tactics varied, but his original purpose of salvation did not.

What was his insistent refrain? "They shall be my people and I shall be their God." He yearns to restore our true identity in authentic relationship. Graciously persistent, he loves and wants to work with and through us, his team. Yet, we failed to live out his original mandate.

Therefore, he eventually sent his Son to make visible his commitment to us and to demonstrate the obedience he desires.

Now, we can see more of the fullness of the Gospel of Jesus and his kingdom. Jesus introduces and embodies his kingdom. Both creation and redemption are in play.

In study 1, we pointed out seven verbs or tasks found in Genesis that are central to our design. These words relate to shaping nature into culture (Genesis 1 and 2): rule; be fruitful; increase; fill; subdue; work; take care of.

We now continue with "seven gifts" of grace that capture the heart of the Gospel. They were presented as the task of the Anointed One in Isaiah

61:1-3 and largely adopted by Jesus in Luke 4:18. They have to do with salvation—transforming sinners into saints: proclamation; healing; liberation; blessing; comfort; hope; renewal.

Although often overlooked, the Gospel is directly connected to God's entrepreneurial motives. Why, after all, is God entrepreneurial? Why did he create the universe and humankind? Why does he care so much about its well-being?

God first demonstrates and declares his good and beautiful designs for life. Then he wants people to be his partners in close relationship with him. Our rejection of him led to tragedy, but the Gospel announces that God has not given up on us. To prove this, and to make a way for us to return to him, he sends his Son. Then he invites us to work with him. Today we are called to be his agents in healing and liberating a broken world.

The implications for us are astonishing. We are not here to hold our breath until heaven. We are here to engage with and contribute to the well-being of the world and the people around us. In this purpose, we find a rich meaning for our work as entrepreneurs. Our businesses can and should be designed to fulfill this high calling of God.

The Gospel of the kingdom orients us to the lordship of Christ in every area of life: education, business, the arts, family, leisure, politics. It embraces both creation and redemption. The present is building on the past, the future is breaking into the present. This Gospel is richly transformative. "Daily life is bursting with theological meaning" (Paul Stevens).

Jesus Christ is our point of integration. He alone can resolve the tensions that originated when we turned away from God. "In him all things hold together" (Colossians 1:17). The thorns and thistles still exist, but we can seek to rejoin God as followers and apprentices on the team of his Son. In the following scriptures, we see God's heart for mending a broken world.

ISAIAH 61:1-3

The Spirit of the Sovereign Lord is on me, because the Lord has anointed me to proclaim good news to the poor. He has sent me to bind up the brokenhearted, to proclaim freedom for the captives and release from darkness for the prisoners, to proclaim the year of the Lord's favor and the day of vengeance of our God, to comfort all who mourn, and provide for those who grieve in Zion—to bestow on them a crown of beauty instead of ashes, the oil of joy instead of mourning, and a garment of praise instead of a spirit of despair. They will be called oaks of righteousness, a planting of the Lord for the display of his splendor.

ISAIAH 58:12

Your people will rebuild the ancient ruins and will raise up the age-old foundations; you will be called Repairer of Broken Walls, Restorer of Streets . . .

JOHN 17:14-18

"I have given them your word and the world has hated them, for they are not of the world any more than I am of the world. My prayer is not that you take them out of the world but that you protect them from the evil one. They are not of the world, even as I am not of it. Sanctify them by the truth; your word is truth. As you sent me into the world, I have sent them into the world."

REVELATION 21:1-5

Then I saw "a new heaven and a new earth," for the first heaven and the first earth had passed away, and there was no longer any sea. I saw the Holy City, the new Jerusalem, coming down out of heaven from God, prepared as a bride beautifully dressed for her husband. And I heard a loud voice from the throne saying, "Look! God's dwelling place is now among the people, and he will dwell with them. They will be his people, and God himself will be with them and be their God. 'He will wipe every tear from their eyes. There will be no more death' or mourning or crying or pain, for the old order of things has passed away." He who was seated on the throne said, "I am making everything new!"

Questions

1. How are you blending the seven tasks and the seven gifts in your daily life as an entrepreneur? As God is seeking to renew the world, how are you participating with him? *Profound Question that takes a lot of thought.*

2. Reflect on the following statement by J. I. Packer: "The Bible teaches that we should plan and live our life as a unity in which nothing is secular and everything is in a real sense sacred, because everything is being done for the glory of God—that is, to show appreciation for what he has made, to please him by loving obedience to his commands, and to advance his honor and praise among his creatures, starting with the homage and adoration that we render to him ourselves. Nothing is to be viewed as less than sacred; there is to be no compartmentalizing of our daily doings; work is to be a unifying reality that holds all our life together."

3. Do you agree with this statement (especially the last sentence)? How does the life of Jesus Christ confirm this unity? *Yes. It is His essence.*

THE GOSPEL AND BUSINESS RELATIONSHIPS

Commerce is a system through which the Gospel can and should flow naturally. As the pioneer William Carey wrote in his *Enquiry* (1792), "Commerce shall serve the Gospel." He assembled a launch team for work in India that included entrepreneurial and business capabilities.

As entrepreneurs, we are occupied with both material and spiritual realities. So was Jesus. This understanding is crucial, as we work in a broken world. The workplace is the setting for most of the stories that Jesus told. The fifty-hour work-week of the marketplace is strategic!

As we have seen, we are called to co-labor with God. This truth should guide and motivate us as we develop enterprises. The idea is elegantly expressed in the Greek term *koinonia,* which usually describes a spiritual partnership in the New Testament. It was commonly in use as a commercial term. Thus, in Luke 5:10, we learn that Peter, James, and John were "partners." They had shares in a fishing business.

Our enterprises are where people can best observe the practical differences that following Jesus produces in our lives. It is here, in our business relationships, that our values and behavior can "make the teaching about God our Savior attractive" (Titus 2:9-10).

To partner with God in the expression of the Gospel through commerce, we must think about more than proclaiming the Gospel with words. We are called to *demonstrate* God's character and love in our relationships and in the excellence of our services and products.

Let's first look at the importance of relationships in business. For example, Paul made it clear that conflict indicates spiritual immaturity. He makes the point that a workplace rife with bullying and backstabbing indicates "worldliness." God needs leaders who imitate Christ in relationships.

1 CORINTHIANS 3:1-4

Brothers and sisters, I could not address you as people who live by the

Spirit but as people who are still worldly—mere infants in Christ. I gave you milk, not solid food, for you were not yet ready for it. Indeed, you are still not ready. You are still worldly. For since there is jealousy and quarreling among you, are you not worldly? Are you not acting like mere humans? For when one says, "I follow Paul," and another, "I follow Apollos," are you not mere human beings?

2 CORINTHIANS 13:11

Strive for full restoration, encourage one another, be of one mind, live in peace. And the God of love and peace will be with you.

HEBREWS 10:24

And let us consider how we may spur one another on toward love and good deeds . . .

EPHESIANS 2:10

For we are God's handiwork, created in Christ Jesus to do good works, which God prepared in advance for us to do.

PHILIPPIANS 2:5-7

In your relationships with one another, have the same mindset as Christ Jesus: Who, being in very nature God, did not consider equality with God something to be used to his own advantage; rather, he made himself nothing by taking the very nature of a servant . . .

Questions

1. What factors contribute to relational conflict? In light of the Scriptures, what helps to instill peace among team members?

self-centeredness
Lack of Trust
Look to Jesus first

A Case Study
Gallup Study on Workplace Relationships

In the 2013 Gallup study titled "State of the American Workplace: Employee Engagement Insights for U.S. Business Leaders," Gallup CEO Jim Clifton expressed concern that "bosses from hell" were causing significant problems for workers. Consider this excerpt from his introduction to the study.

At Gallup, we've studied the impact of human nature on the economy for decades. We've now reviewed more than twenty-five million responses to our employee engagement survey. And what we found out about managers and employees has serious implications for the future of American companies and the world. Of the approximately 100 million people in America who hold full-time jobs, thirty million (30 percent) are engaged and inspired at work, so we can assume they have a great boss. At the other end of the spectrum are roughly twenty million (20 percent) employees who are actively disengaged. These employees, who have bosses from hell that make them miserable, roam the halls spreading discontent. The other fifty million (50 percent) American workers are not engaged. They're just kind of present, but not inspired by their work or their managers. . . . Gallup research also shows that these managers from hell are creating active disengagement costing the U.S. an estimated $450 billion to $550 billion annually. If your company reflects the average in the U.S., just imagine what poor management and disengagement are costing your bottom line. On the other hand, imagine if your company doubled the number of great managers and engaged employees. Gallup finds that the thirty million engaged employees in the U.S. come up with most of the innovative ideas, create most of a company's new customers, and have the most entrepreneurial energy.

As an entrepreneur, what is your responsibility in creating a healthy relational culture at work? When it comes to disengaged workers, what factors beyond the managers might be at play? What practical ideas do you have for improving the situation?

THE GOSPEL AND OUR PRODUCTS AND SERVICES

Another powerful way to help the Gospel flow through our enterprises is to develop excellent products and services. We want to be in the world as salt: scattered, engaged, relevant, and restorative. We should aim to be quality leaders as well as moral leaders—to exceed expectations. Therefore, whatever our product or service, we should strive to make it "good" just as God demonstrated in his creation. "Let us not become weary in doing good, for at the proper time we will reap a harvest if we do not give up" (Galatians 6:9). Or, as Titus 3:14 says, "Our people must learn to devote themselves to doing what is good, in order to provide for urgent needs and not live unproductive lives."

Righteousness and justice are the foundations of the kingdom (Psalm 89:14). This should shape our decisions to allocate the resources we generate among such uses as setting aside reserves, building the enterprise, leveraging economic power, creating more jobs, resisting injustice, serving the poor and vulnerable, and living more comfortably. We see in Matthew 25 that the king will divide us into sheep and goats according to how we have seen him and responded in the lives of those who are needy—those whom Jesus calls "the least of these brothers of mine" (verse 40).

Let's take what is perhaps a surprising example of a Christian entrepreneur, the Irish brewer Arthur Guinness (1725-1803). He was led by God to adopt the mission, "make a drink that men will drink that will be good for them." Too heavy to get drunk on easily, Guinness Stout reduced alcoholism on the streets of Ireland and lessened the "gin craze." Christians drank beer as a statement of moderation. Many of the best breweries were founded by Christians. Guinness led the way with fair and generous practices for his employees, built homes for the poor and homeless, fed the hungry, and accomplished significant changes in the British legal system. He was a good friend of William Wilberforce, the British political leader who led the charge to abolish slavery. Other Christian entrepreneurs who founded UK companies with a strong holistic vision to serve the disadvantaged included the so-called "Chocolate Trinity" of Cadbury, Fry, and Rowntree.

Enterprises should generate wealth and help meet the physical needs of a society. They are vital in tackling poverty and restoring hope. They leverage capital. They can contribute to economic justice and stand against corruption.

God prompted Jeremiah to write to the Jews whom Nebuchadnezzar had deported to Babylon. They were refugees, forced to labor in the very center of enemy territory, miserably displaced. Astonishingly, God urged his people to integrate with the enemy—to become "insiders"—to bring *shalom* (peace and prosperity) to our cultures.

As we see in the scriptures below, our products and services should be expressions of God's desire for goodness, justice, and love.

PSALM 89:14

Righteousness and justice are the foundation of your throne; love and faithfulness go before you.

MATTHEW 25:37-46

"Then the righteous will answer him, 'Lord, when did we see you hungry and feed you, or thirsty and give you something to drink? When did we see you a stranger and invite you in, or needing clothes and clothe you? When did we see you sick or in prison and go to visit you?'

"The King will reply, 'Truly I tell you, whatever you did for one of the least of these brothers and sisters of mine, you did for me.'

"Then he will say to those on his left, 'Depart from me, you who are cursed, into the eternal fire prepared for the devil and his angels. For I was hungry and you gave me nothing to eat, I was thirsty and you gave me nothing to drink, I was a stranger and you did not invite me in, I needed clothes and you did not clothe me, I was sick and in prison and you did not look after me.'

"They also will answer, 'Lord, when did we see you hungry or thirsty or a stranger or needing clothes or sick or in prison, and did not help you?'

"He will reply, 'Truly I tell you, whatever you did not do for one of the least of these, you did not do for me.' Then they will go away to eternal punishment, but the righteous to eternal life."

MATTHEW 25:14-27

"Again, it will be like a man going on a journey, who called his servants and entrusted his wealth to them. To one he gave five bags of gold, to another two bags, and to another one bag, each according to his ability. Then he went on his journey. The man who had received five bags of gold went at once and put his money to work and gained five bags more. So also, the one with two bags of gold gained two more. But the man who had received one bag went off, dug a hole in the ground and hid his master's money.

"After a long time the master of those servants returned and settled accounts with them. The man who had received five bags of gold brought the other five. 'Master,' he said, 'you entrusted me with five bags of gold. See, I have gained five more.'

"His master replied, 'Well done, good and faithful servant! You have been faithful with a few things; I will put you in charge of many things.

Come and share your master's happiness!'

"The man with two bags of gold also came. 'Master,' he said, 'you entrusted me with two bags of gold; see, I have gained two more.'

"His master replied, 'Well done, good and faithful servant! You have been faithful with a few things; I will put you in charge of many things. Come and share your master's happiness!'

"Then the man who had received one bag of gold came. 'Master,' he said, 'I knew that you are a hard man, harvesting where you have not sown and gathering where you have not scattered seed. So I was afraid and went out and hid your gold in the ground. See, here is what belongs to you.'

"His master replied, 'You wicked, lazy servant! So you knew that I harvest where I have not sown and gather where I have not scattered seed? Well then, you should have put my money on deposit with the bankers, so that when I returned I would have received it back with interest."

JEREMIAH 29:4-9

This is what the Lord Almighty, the God of Israel, says to all those I carried into exile from Jerusalem to Babylon: "Build houses and settle down; plant gardens and eat what they produce. Marry and have sons and daughters; find wives for your sons and give your daughters in marriage, so that they too may have sons and daughters. Increase in number there; do not decrease. Also, seek the peace and prosperity of the city to which I have carried you into exile. Pray to the Lord for it, because if it prospers, you too will prosper. " Yes, this is what the Lord Almighty, the God of Israel, says: "Do not let the prophets and diviners among you deceive you. Do not listen to the dreams you encourage them to have. They are prophesying lies to you in my name. I have not sent them," declares the Lord.

Questions

1. What do these scriptures suggest about our responsibilities in the midst of "a crooked and depraved generation" (Philippians 2:15)?

2. Most entrepreneurs must consider "market demand" as they make business decisions and consider profitability. Does market demand conflict with or cooperate with our calling to develop products and services that bring *shalom* to people?

3. People flourish when we can integrate the tasks of our mandate and the gifts of the Gospel in the setting of the kingdom. It is often not easy, but the question remains: How do proclamation and presence, word and deed, combine to lift up Jesus Christ in your enterprise?

A Case Study
The Bible and Technology

Excerpt from *The Book That Made Your World,* by Vishal Mangalwadi

What accelerated Western technological progress in the

Middle Ages? That question was the topic of a 1961 Oxford Symposium on Scientific Change, spearheaded by Alistair Crombie. The best answer was given by Marburg historian Ernst Benz, who published a seminal essay in 1964, *"Fondamenti Christiani della Tecnica Occidentale."* It demonstrated that "Christian beliefs provided the rationale, and faith, and motive energy for Western technology."

. . . Christendom pioneered technological creativity because the Bible presented a God who was a Creator, neither a dreamer nor a dancer, as Indian sages believed. God was the *architect* of the cosmos. He shaped man out of clay as a potter does, making man in his own creative image and commanding him to rule the world creatively.

Jesus Christ's incarnation in a physical body and his bodily resurrection instilled into Christian philosophers the unique idea that matter was created for a spiritual purpose.

. . . Benz realized that the Judeo-Christian view of reality and destiny produced and nurtured technology in four ways: First, the Bible emphasized intelligent craftsmanship in the world's design. Second, the Bible suggested that human beings participate in divine workmanship by being good artisans themselves. Third, the Bible taught that we follow divine example when we use the physical universe for righteous ends. And fourth, the Bible challenged the West to use time wisely, because each moment is a valuable, one-time opportunity.

. . . The biblical idea of new birth included a reorientation of the will to do good works. This moral activism combined with a strong biblical work ethic proved conducive to promoting humanizing and liberating technology.

Benz says that the Christian worldview promoted humanizing technology in four ways. To what extent do these four factors motivate technological innovation today? How do they influence *your* business plans?

CORPORATE CULTURE AND THE GOSPEL

How does the culture of your business align with the Gospel?

Although this question deserves an entire study, in this section we will focus on the need to create a corporate culture in which every employee, regardless of his or her responsibility in the company, is treated with dignity.

Recent studies reveal that most American workers are struggling at work because of poor workplace relationships. In addition to the Gallup research mentioned earlier in this book, many people don't believe that their work is valuable to their employers. They believe that those "at the top" do the important work and those at the "bottom" are just "grunts." This notion is not biblical. The idea of a hierarchy of occupations came from prominent Greek thinkers, such as Plato, not from the Scriptures. Yet it has infected us deeply.

It is liberating to absorb Paul's instruction in 1 Corinthians 12:4-7: "There are different kinds of gifts (*charisma*), but the same Spirit distributes them. There are different kinds of service (*diakonia*), but the same Lord. There are different kinds of working (*energema*), but in all of them and in everyone it is the same God at work. Now to each one the manifestation of the Spirit is given for the common good."

There is no hierarchy of occupations, in the sense that some are more "spiritual" or closer to the heart of God than others. We have to qualify this, of course, by rejecting work that promotes sin: for example, generating political lies (propaganda) or sexual lust (pornography). However, a large question remains: Are some valid occupations more contributory than others? Contributory to what? Are some acceptable products more trivial than others? Should we distinguish satisfying desires from meeting needs? In our disordered and unjust world, is the marketing of hula hoops and mosquito nets of similar moral value? If not, what criteria should distinguish among occupations?

The Scriptures help us with this question. Our model is the mutual love of the three persons of our triune God. The daily language that we use in conducting our enterprises contains echoes of this relationality, which is often expressed in the New Testament using the metaphor of a body with interconnected parts that each serve a different function, Paul's metaphor of the *Corpus Christi* or Body of Christ.

The word "corporation" is derived from the Latin root for "a body." It refers to persons authorized to act as one body. The word points to the relational character of business. Indeed, a business is a strategic opportunity to reflect the relationality of God himself. Our triune God is relational, hospitable, interdependent, social—our model for purposeful community. As Wayne Grudem writes in *Business for the Glory of God,* "In buying and selling we also manifest interdependence and thus reflect the interdependence and interpersonal love among the members of the Trinity." It is "God, who makes things grow" (1 Corinthians 3:7), and we are on his team.

Similarly, the word "company" is derived from two Latin roots: *com* and *panis,* "together" and "bread." Hence, it meant associates or companions close enough to share meals together.

The coming of Jesus Christ restored dignity to work and brought fresh significance to us as workers. Because we are committed to Christ, we are also committed to work with a purpose, knowing "that the creation itself will be liberated from its bondage to decay and brought into the freedom and glory of the children of God" (Romans 8:21). Carrying out our work in faith, hope, and love continues the work of Christ himself. As stated in 1 Thessalonians 1:2-3, "We always thank God for all of you and continually mention you in our prayers. We remember before our God and Father your work produced by faith, your labor prompted by love, and your endurance inspired by hope in our Lord Jesus Christ."

We do not deny the drudgery of work, but we can transform it into redemptive service through Christ's rejuvenating power within us. Despite our brokenness, we can aspire to work in Christ's image for God's glory. And, as business leaders, we have a high calling to create business cultures that enable people to flourish.

Because corporate cultures are often mere "grist mills" where workers don't thrive, we have an opportunity to bring renewal. "Redemption" is a term from the marketplace: a commercial transaction, a buying back of what was lost or in bondage to another master. A redeemer does for others what they are unable to do for themselves. He restores their place and their identity. In the New Testament, redemption is spoken of as paying a ransom and as extending to us the forgiveness that we cannot arrange for ourselves through the sacrificial death of Jesus Christ. Purchased out of slavery to sin, we are adopted into the family of God. Does your enterprise "redeem" people?

"Salvation" is a rich and capacious term in the New Testament. For example, in the Gospels the Greek verb *sozein* is used for physical healing and for spiritual salvation. The apostle Peter begins his first letter with insights that tell us that our salvation is past and present and future. Eugene Peterson, in *Reversed Thunder,* has an apt comment regarding salvation.

> The root meaning in Hebrew of "salvation" is to be broad, to become spacious, to enlarge. It carries the sense of deliverance from an existence that has become compressed, confined, and cramped...Salvation is God's determination to rescue his creation; it is his activity in recovering the world. It is personal and impersonal, it deals with souls and cities, it touches sin and sickness. There is a reckless indiscriminateness about salvation.

Questions

1. Does your work contribute to God's intent of salvation? Why or why not?

2. What creative ideas do you have for improving business cultures? Can entrepreneurs *impose* changes in business culture?

Yes

Quotations

"If you are a manual laborer, you will find the Bible has been put into your workshop, into your hand, into your heart. It teaches and preaches how you should treat your neighbor . . . just look at your tools . . . at your needle and thimble, your beer bottle, your goods, your scales . . . everything our bodies do, the external and the carnal, is and is called spiritual behavior if God's Word is added to it and it is done in faith" (Martin Luther, 1483-1546).

"If you are called to be a street sweeper, sweep streets even as Michelangelo painted or Beethoven composed music or Shakespeare wrote poetry. Sweep streets so well that all the hosts of heaven and earth will pause to say, 'here lived a great street sweeper who did his job well'" (Martin Luther King, Jr., 1929-1968).

"My father is a seller of fish. We children know the business too, having worked from childhood in the Great South Bay Fish Market on Long Island, New York, helping our father like a quiver full of arrows. It is a small store, and it smells like fish . . . my father is in full-time service for the Lord: prophet, priest, and king in the fish business. And customers who come to the store sense it. Not that we always have the cheapest fish in town! Not that there are no mistakes on a busy Friday morning! Not that there is no sin! But that little Great South Bay Fish Market, my father and two employees, is not only a clean, honest place where you can buy quality fish at a reasonable price with a smile, but there is a spirit in the store, a spirit of laughter, of fun, of joy inside the buying and selling that strikes an observer pleasantly; and the strenuous week-long preparations in the back rooms for Friday fish-day are not a routine drudgery inter-rupted by "rest periods," but again, a spirit seems to hallow the lowly work into a rich service, in which it is good to officiate. When I watch my dad's hands, big beefy hands with broad stubby fingers each twice the thickness of mine . . . when I watch those hands delicately split the back of a mack-erel or with a swift, true stroke fillet a flounder close to the bone, leav-ing all the meat together . . . twinkling at work without complaint, past temptations, struggling day in and day out to fix a just price, in weakness often but always in faith consecratedly cutting up fish before the face of the Lord: when I see that, I know God's grace can come down to a man's hand and the flash of a scabby fish knife" (Calvin Seerveld, as told to Paul Marshall in *Heaven Is Not my Home*).

"Unfortunately, many of the available jobs in our economy are geared to the production and sale of that which is cheap, frivolous, environmen-tally hazardous, and socially unsound. Our highly commercialized culture is filled with goods and services of dubious value. And the techniques of modern advertising have proven lamentably effective in generating a de-mand for them. Simply having the right attitude, the 'Christian attitude,' toward one's work is not enough. One must also take into consideration the social content of one's work. Am I, in my job, making a positive contri-bution to the human community; am I helping to meet legitimate human needs; am I somehow enhancing or promoting what is true, what is noble, and what is worthy in human life?" (Lee Hardy, *The Fabric of this World*).

"For we are God's handiwork, created in Christ Jesus to do good works, which God prepared in advance for us to do" (Ephesians 2:10).

"Servants, respectfully obey your earthly masters but always with an eye to obeying the *real* master, Christ. Don't just do what you have to do to get by, but work heartily, as Christ's servants doing what God wants you to do. And work with a smile on your face, always keeping in mind that no matter who happens to be giving the orders, you're really serving God. Good work will get you good pay from the Master, regardless of whether you are slave or free" (Ephesians 6:5-8, *The Message*).

"Theology and economics do not inhabit separate universes but combine in the biblical experience and practice of redemption" (Christopher Wright, *The Mission of God's People*).

"I simply argue that the cross be raised again at the center of the marketplace as well as on the steeple of the church. I am recovering the claim that Jesus was not crucified in a cathedral between two candles, but on a cross between two thieves; on the town garbage heap; at a crossroad so cosmopolitan that they had to write his title in Hebrew and in Latin and in Greek . . . at the kind of place where cynics talk smut and thieves curse and soldiers gamble" (George MacLeod, 1895-1991, founder of the Iona Community).

"In writing about the ministry of the state (in Romans 13:4-6), Paul twice uses the very same word which he has used elsewhere of the ministers of the church. . . . *Diakonia* is a generic term which can embrace a wide variety of ministries. Those who serve the state as legislators, civil servants, magistrates, police, social workers, or tax-collectors are just as much 'ministers of God' as those who serve the church as pastors, teachers, evangelists or administrators" (John Stott, 1921-2011, *The Message of Romans*).

THE CULMINATION OF ENTERPRISES

Viewpoint of this Study:

God, the Satisfied Entrepreneur
Overcoming – Completing – Celebrating

The kingdom, or reign, of God may also be thought of reverently as the enterprise of God, the working out on a cosmic scale of his eternal "purpose and grace, which was given us in Christ Jesus before the beginning of time, but has now been revealed through the appearing of our Savior, Christ Jesus, who has destroyed death and has brought life and immortality to light through the Gospel" (2 Timothy 1:9-10).

Though the kingdom of God is the central and enduring expression of the Father's intent that "in everything he [Christ] might have the supremacy" (Colossians 1:18), it is worth observing that the notion of God's "enterprise" offers fertile soil for interpreting his program to a generation saturated in materialism. Here is the one unblemished enterprise!

The Father's "good pleasure, which he purposed in Christ . . . [is] to bring unity to all things in heaven and on earth under Christ" (Ephesians 1:9-10). The climax of history is that earth and heaven will finally be united, integrated, and whole. The Holy City comes down out of the heavens, so that "God's dwelling place is now among the people, and he will dwell with them." Everything will be refreshed, and reconstituted (Revelation 21:2-5).

REVELATION 21:2-4

I saw the Holy City, the new Jerusalem, coming down out of heaven from God, prepared as a bride beautifully dressed for her husband. And I heard a loud voice from the throne saying, "Look! God's dwelling place is now among the people, and he will dwell with them. . . . 'He will wipe every tear from their eyes. There will be no more death' or mourning or crying or pain, for the old order of things has passed away."

ROMANS 8:18-25

I consider that our present sufferings are not worth comparing with the glory that will be revealed in us. For the creation waits in eager expectation for the children of God to be revealed. For the creation was subjected to frustration, not by its own choice, but by the will of the one who subjected it, in hope that the creation itself will be liberated from its bondage to decay and brought into the freedom and glory of the children of God. We know that the whole creation has been groaning as in the pains of childbirth right up to the present time. Not only so, but we ourselves, who have the first-fruits of the Spirit, groan inwardly as we wait eagerly for our adoption as sons, the redemption of our bodies. For in this hope we were saved. But hope that is seen is no hope at all. Who hopes for what they already have? But if we hope for what we do not yet have, we wait for it patiently.

ISAIAH 32:15-18

. . . till the Spirit is poured on us from on high, and the desert becomes a fertile field, and the fertile field seems like a forest. The Lord's justice will dwell in the desert, his righteousness live in the fertile field. The fruit of that righteousness will be peace; its effect will be quietness and confidence forever. My people will live in peaceful dwelling places, in secure homes, in undisturbed places of rest.

Questions

1. The scriptures above demonstrate that our ultimate salvation depends on God's work, not on human effort. In our modern cultures, to what extent do we base our identity and hope in our professional and commercial success?

Most of us do that.
I did for a long time.
I can still do that if I am not vigilante.

A VISION OF ULTIMATE SUCCESS

Paul points out that the offspring of Abraham will be heirs of the world (the *kosmos,* Romans 4:13), not merely of the land. There will be total celebration in which all of creation joins. "Let the heavens rejoice, let the earth be glad" (Psalm 96:11). Similarly, Isaiah 11:1-10 pictures a reconstructed world and people, infused with the Spirit, thriving under a perfect king.

ROMANS 4:13

It was not through the law that Abraham and his offspring received the promise that he would be heir of the world, but through the righteousness that comes by faith.

PSALM 96:11-13

Let the heavens rejoice, let the earth be glad; let the sea resound, and all that is in it. Let the fields be jubilant, and everything in them; let all the trees of the forest sing for joy. Let all creation rejoice before the Lord, for he comes, he comes to judge the earth. He will judge the world in righteousness and the peoples in his faithfulness.

ISAIAH 11:1-10

A shoot will come up from the stump of Jesse; from his roots a

Branch will bear fruit. The Spirit of the Lord will rest on him—the Spirit of wisdom and of understanding, the Spirit of counsel and of might, the Spirit of the knowledge and fear of the Lord—and he will delight in the fear of the Lord. He will not judge by what he sees with his eyes, or decide by what he hears with his ears; but with righteousness he will judge the needy, with justice he will give decisions for the poor of the earth. He will strike the earth with the rod of his mouth; with the breath of his lips he will slay the wicked. Righteousness will be his belt and faithfulness the sash around his waist. The wolf will live with the lamb, the leopard will lie down with the goat, the calf and the lion and the yearling together; and a little child will lead them. The cow will feed with the bear, their young will lie down together, and the lion will eat straw like the ox. . . . for the earth will be filled with the knowledge of the Lord as the waters cover the sea. In that day the Root of Jesse will stand as a banner for the peoples; the nations will rally to him, and his resting place will be glorious.

Questions

1. How should the eternal promises of God, our ultimate salvation, influence the way we think about the lasting meaning of our enterprises and work? *We should consider what it is that our businesses do that will last.*

Impact on people. → Do that well.

WORK THAT IS NEVER IN VAIN

Paul's great statement about our resurrection in 1 Corinthians 15 tells us that our natural bodies will be raised as spiritual bodies and our mortal must be clothed with immortality (verses 44 and 53).

Therefore he concludes, "your labor in the Lord is not in vain" (verse 58). Earlier he tells the Corinthians that we should be careful how we build because our work will be exposed and, if what we have built survives, we will receive our reward(1 Corinthians 3:10-15).

1 CORINTHIANS 15:44, 50-58

. . . it is sown a natural body, it is raised a spiritual body. If there is a natural body, there is also a spiritual body. . . . I declare to you, brothers and sisters, that flesh and blood cannot inherit the kingdom of God, nor does the perishable inherit the imperishable. Listen, I tell you a mystery: We will not all sleep, but we will all be changed— in a flash, in the twinkling of an eye, at the last trumpet. For the trumpet will sound, the dead will be raised imperishable, and we will be changed. For the perishable must clothe itself with the imperishable, and the mortal with immortality. When the perishable has been clothed with the imperishable, and the mortal with immortality, then the saying that is written will come true: "Death has been swallowed up in victory."

"Where, O death, is your victory? Where, O death, is your sting?" The sting of death is sin, and the power of sin is the law. But thanks be to God! He gives us the victory through our Lord Jesus Christ. Therefore, my dear brothers and sisters, stand firm. Let nothing move you. Always give yourselves fully to the work of the Lord, because you know that your labor in the Lord is not in vain.

1 CORINTHIANS 3:10-15

By the grace God has given me, I laid a foundation as a wise builder, and someone else is building on it. But each one should build with care. For no one can lay any foundation other than the one already laid, which is Jesus Christ. If anyone builds on this foundation using gold, silver, costly stones, wood, hay or straw, their work will be shown for what it is, because the Day will bring it to light. It will be revealed with fire, and the fire will test the quality of each person's work. If what has been built survives, the builder will receive a reward. If it is burned up, the builder will suffer loss but yet will be saved—even though only as one escaping through the flames.

Questions

1. In 1 Corinthians 15, Paul states that the work of Jesus on the cross and his resurrection fill our lives with meaning. How should this impact our work? Why do you think Paul says "your labor in the Lord is not in vain"?

We are to build up treasure in heaven.

THE TRIUMPH OF THE KING

The tragedy of our failure is finally reversed at the end of time. Chapters 20-22 of Revelation describe the triumph of our king, the eviction of Satan, the end of pain and mourning and death. The God who drummed us out of the Garden of Eden is the one who welcomes us into his Holy City. The tree of life returns and the darkness ends. "They will see his face" and "the Lord God will give them light" (Revelation 22:4-5). Read Revelation 20-22 for a more complete view of God's ultimate victory.

The Greek word translated "new" in 2 Peter 3 and Revelation 21 is no *neos,* which means completely new, but *kainos,* which means new in nature or quality. Thus, the universe that has been divinely renewed will stand in real continuity with our present heaven and earth.

The Scriptures tell us that we are destined for a city—the new Jerusalem—at the intersection of heaven and earth, a city "whose architect and builder is God" (Hebrews 11:10).

ISAIAH 65:17-25

See, I will create new heavens and a new earth. The former things will not be remembered, nor will they come to mind. But be glad and rejoice forever in what I will create, for I will create Jerusalem to be a delight and its people a joy. I will rejoice over Jerusalem and take delight in my people; the sound of weeping and of crying will be heard in it no more. "Never again will there be in it an infant who lives but a few days, or an old man who does not live out his years; the one who dies at a hundred will be thought a mere child; the one who fails to reach a hundred will be considered accursed. They will build houses and dwell in them; they will plant vineyards and eat their fruit. No longer will they build houses and others live in them, or plant and others eat. For as the days of a tree, so will be the days of my people; my chosen ones will long enjoy the work of their hands. They will not labor in vain, nor will they bear children doomed to misfortune; for they will be a people blessed by the Lord, they and their descendants with them. Before they call I will answer; while they are still speaking I will hear. The wolf and the lamb will feed together, and the lion will eat straw like the ox, and dust will be the serpent's food. They will neither harm nor destroy on all my holy mountain," says the Lord.

Questions

1. Within the setting of the *shalom* of the created order, for which creation groans as it waits, Isaiah's vision includes construction and agriculture (verse 21). How will the way in which such occupations are practiced differ from what we have experienced since the Industrial Revolution?

We will build with our hands and for ourselves. - Not others

DESTROYING THE LAST ENEMY

We live among the ruptured relationships that permeate commerce. Yet, in the days to come, our anonymous modern gaps between producers and consumers, our isolation and competition will dissolve into transformed community. Joy, health, and generational blessing await us. The curse will be lifted and we will reign with him in his city. Because the last enemy to be destroyed is death, only then will we be entering into the fullness of a *shalom,* which we can now only experience in part. *Shalom* brings inner serenity and calm. It is when our soul prospers. It comes when we are in harmony. When we experience the fullness of *shalom,* we will be spiritually and emotionally healthy. We will be whole—rightly related to God and his creation. We will at last be living according to God's specification.

Moreover, the Spirit tells us in Revelation 14:13 that those who die in the Lord are blessed because "they will rest from their labor, for their deeds (*erga*) will follow them." These, it seems, are the deeds that God originally designed us to pursue and that are later redeemed.

REVELATION 21:22-27

I did not see a temple in the city, because the Lord God Almighty and the Lamb are its temple. The city does not need the sun or the moon to shine on it, for the glory of God gives it light, and the Lamb is its lamp. The nations will walk by its light, and the kings of the earth will bring their splendor in to it. On no day will gates ever be shut, for there will be no night there. The glory and honor of the nations will be brought into it. Nothing impure will ever enter it, nor will anyone who does what is shameful or deceitful, but only those whose names are written in the Lamb's book of life.

Questions

1. What does Revelation 21:22-27 suggest about the destination of God's grand enterprise? What will happen to our enterprises?

CONCLUSION

Because the earth is the Lord's and everything in it (Psalm 24:1); because God uses the marvels of creation to demonstrate his divinity; because everything he created is good (1 Timothy 4:4); because he sent his Son to restore the world, not merely people; because of all this, much of our disordered world will surely be put right rather than obliterated. God will transform swords into plows.

Our mandate was and is to "fill" the earth, to turn nature into culture. We turned aside to try to build a flawed city that could reach heaven (Genesis 11:1-8), but instead we are to receive God's city coming down to grace us and receive our offerings of the best of our "fillings."

Few people think of business or commerce as morally good in itself. Yet, it can be a splendid arena in which to reflect God's character in the conduct of our daily affairs. Clearly, a "good" enterprise profitably supplies products or services that are needed and that are well-constructed. Integrity prevails, employees flourish, creativity is celebrated, customers are blessed, stakeholders are contributing, and resources are multiplied. Too often, we have harnessed God's provision of a capital base to rebellious uses, idolatrous functions, and selfish ends. God will judge us. But he will invite into his city both us and the best of the "fillings" that we have faithfully stewarded. Zion will be a magnetic city (Isaiah 60:4-8). The light of the Lamb will illuminate and judge and heal us and our productions.

Questions

1. What should a "good" enterprise produce or generate—good in a similar sense to what God produced in his original launch? What do you desire as the ultimate fate of your enterprise?

Quotations

"We commit ourselves without reserve to all the secular work our shared humanity requires of us, knowing that nothing we do in itself is good enough to form part of that city's (the New Jerusalem) building, knowing that everything . . . is part of that sin-stained human nature that must go down into the valley of death and judgment, and yet knowing that as we offer it up to the Father in the name of Jesus and in the power of the Spirit, it is safe with him and —purged in fire—it will find its place in the holy city at the end" (Lesslie Newbigin, 1909-1998).

"Every act of love, gratitude, and kindness; every work of art or music inspired by the love of God and delight in the beauty of his creation; every minute spent teaching a severely handicapped child to read or to walk; every act of care and nurture . . . every deed that spreads the Gospel, builds up the church, embraces and embodies holiness rather than corruption, and makes the name of Jesus honored in the world—all of this will find its way, through the resurrecting power of God, into the new creation that God will one day make" (N. T. Wright, *Surprised by Hope*).

"Christian hope, therefore, is for a full, recreated life in the presence and love of God, a totally renewed creation, an integrated new heavens and new earth, and a complete humanness . . . complete in worship and love for God, complete in love for one another as humans, complete in stewardship over God's world" (N. T. Wright, *New Heavens, New Earth*).

"The 'splendor,' 'glory,' and 'honor' of kings and nations is the combined product of generations of human beings whose lives and efforts will have generated the vast store of human cultures and civilizations. In other words, what will be brought into the great city of God in the new creation will be the vast accumulated output of human work through the ages. All this will be purged, redeemed, and laid at the feet of Christ, for the enhancement of the life of eternity in the new creation. Does that not transform our perspective on a Monday morning?" (Christopher Wright, *The Mission of God's People*).

ADDITIONAL BOOKS BY GCN AUTHORS

The Scriptural Roots of Commerce

Used by small groups of business professionals around the world, the *Scriptural Roots of Commerce* (SRC) is a series designed to stimulate conversations about business and economics. The SRC titles are:

- *Why God Matters*: Our view of God shapes our view of work.
- *Why People Matter:* the purpose of commerce is people.
- *Life in the Kingdom*: work in the context of God's purposes.
- *Working Together*: principles for workplace relationships.
- *The Meaning of Work*: theology of work, innovation, and rest.
- *The Economy of God:* a new perspective on wealth and economics.
- *Facilitator's Guide*: practical help for leading small groups through the SRC.

Wealth and Wisdom: A Biblical Perspective on Economics

Written by business entrepreneur Jake Barnett, this book provides a practical theology of capital, economic systems, generosity, and finance.

All titles can be purchased on Amazon in print or digital formats.
For more information, see www.globalcommercenetwork.com

Made in United States
North Haven, CT
19 February 2023